Aggregate of disturbances

Aggregate of disturbances

POEMS BY

Michele Glazer

University of Iowa Press
Iowa City

University of Iowa Press, Iowa City 52242
Printed in the United States of America
http://www.uiowa.edu/uiowapress

The publication of this book was generously
supported by the University of Iowa Foundation.

Printed on acid-free paper

Library of Congress
Cataloging-in-Publication Data
Glazer, Michele.
Aggregate of disturbances: poems / by Michele Glazer.
p.   cm.—(The Iowa poetry prize)
ISBN 0-87745-878-2 (pbk.)
I. Title. II. Series.
PS3557.L388A74   2004
811'.54—dc22   2003063407

04 05 06 07 08 P 5 4 3 2 1

For Ursula

Contents

Acknowledgments

I thank the following journals in which some of these poems first appeared: *Colorado Review*, "Inscape," "Matter," "box," "Real Life #14: Vagaries"; *Delmar*, "Historic House, Astoria," "The Infinite Imperative," "Sonnet," "Valediction"; *Field*, "Lament," "2 Blinds & a Bittern," "Letter," "Home Is a Stone House"; *Harvard Review*, "Echo to Narcissus"; *Volt*, "Translucencies, her death," "The Fecundity"; *Windfall*, "Early Romance: Japanese Garden *(in the heart of the city)*," "A Small Infidelity."

Grateful acknowledgment to James Lavadour for the use of his stunning painting and to Bruce Guenther and Amanda Ham of the Portland Art Museum for their assistance.

Generous grants from the National Endowment for the Arts, the Regional Arts and Culture Council, and Literary Arts, Inc., helped me complete this book.

My thanks especially to Claudia Bischoff, Brian Gard, Laura Mullen, and Patricia Staton for their helpful comments over many years and for their own inspiring work; Steve Tilden, my multifarious collaborator; my family for their support and all else; and John Laursen—his fine eye.

Aggregate of **disturbances**

2 Blinds & a Bittern

Among bitterns one is blind.
Among reeds, bittern is the middle swayer.
In the blind I am all eyes.
To the eye on the other side I am
abstract, an eye, too, and green
but nothing
to beat your wings about.

The blind offered itself as a way to see
deeper into what out there
kept at abeyance, us.
Still, when we were happy we forgot ourselves . . . . . . something like that.
Who watches for what moves
and what sits
still among the rushes?
And where the branch
meets the bird.
I didn't say I was interested in the birds, particularly,
I just said I couldn't find them.

In the blind we are all eyes and I
am the middle swayer.
In the blind we pull birds out of the sky with other birds
we work *like puppets*
into the net between the firs.
This blind runs Cooper's hawks —

the blind with the rain gutter and the burlap-covered boards.
There is concern about the bird whose tail lacks rigidity.
The lure-birds ride pulleys — pigeon, dove, English sparrow.
They wear leather vests and precious little else.

Someone bolts for the caught hawk, checks it for crop, for molt, for parasites,
the wing pit for fat. Opens the hatch.

It's easy to love a thing against the sky but you can't just look at one thing and say,
"oh, it's a redtail."   *It has to all add up.*

Wherein space is constructed that matter may reside in . . .

The weather forecast that snow would fall from the sky.

(The architecture of snow was like the architecture

of the storm itself, and of the landscape.)

The weather forecast *was* that snow would fall.

We are like snow he said.

She understood her heart was cold.

And that if the walls could not be breached by rhetoric

or conjecture, still they leaned, comfortably

perhaps, one against the other,

an aggregate of disturbances, rust

that in the meantime corrodes, makes beautiful.

You are like snow. She thought,

but I told you that before.

The architecture of loss, the hand of a loved one.

You are not like other weather he said.

Matter

i

The pronghorn's all four legs had caught in the fence & it had worn one
   side of its face
smooth in the dirt trying to separate its flesh from the barbed wire.
   It was moving
& if the struggle was for the mother whose footprint we had seen earlier
   or for the juniper
here & there or the vastness of sagebrush it was also about pain
   & the certainty
of metal that seized as the animal shrank against large birds circling in
   the sky & coyotes
& from the sun. Anyone looking down would have wondered
that the animal should fear things circling & round. By *worn its face smooth*
I mean rubbed the hair off.

It had been all day without water & the dirt, too, is worn smooth here
   where the head rubbed
over it.

It wasn't a pronghorn but an elk & the eye was clear water silted over &
   the shape of itself.
It was the content of another.

Then it is back to the garden, you see, where everything grows
with such fecundity (witness the rampant mint) that she must be
constantly pulling up & putting everything into it & everything
has begun to feel like

more, putting herself into it.

ii

The comeupon head of the baby goat was glossy white, a kind of third-
world neon because this was Kathmandu & walking by looking back
didn't clarify whether it was the real head or why its eyes looked
moist but I got it

the head that had been part of the animal — now a window
advertisement for its own dismembered parts.

A Small Infidelity

The stalk was knocked flat & the allium's great lavender sphere
kissed the dirt & in the aftermath the pendulous blossomed
tip bobbed like a wand madly attempting to enchant — enchant — enchant.

I wanted to believe that it happened to amuse me.

Madly, with decreasing
frequency.

Then another stalk hit the ground
in a motion too eccentric to be the wind.

Okay, then.

From where I stood at the basement window clearly
nature had determined to show itself whimsical.
Or something too delicious lived in there.

Ants?

The bird seemed to lack consequences.
The bird seemed to explain everything.

Surely something is wanted that will not supplicate under
sparrowweight

though for a moment it rested its body on a sphere of blossoms
as he had wrested assumption from the lightness of her words.

Firefly

At his lips
Intact — quick-lit —
And illumination
Dims now
Tell me again

What it was you meant to say

box

rather a box of winds
than a sack, then

my heart's carapace.
am rust. anointed

danger, nature, lust.
rather for what?

am stall, then.
rather, a sack of winds.

who trusts in god knows
dumb luck's

other half
that startles, starts.

inside the box the god in truss.
rather the river than the rock

the river breaks on
that sack of winds, like something

I whispered into
your ear nothing

was said.

On *So*

So,

the navigational
show-

stopper, cliff-

singer,
the *let's not go into this.*

So   and so I thought
because would follow.

We will die so we are human
but we are human for we will die,

isn't it beautiful, hasn't it lasted

Translucencies, her death

I couldn't imagine it so I couldn't believe it.

That ragging absence. That thing inside her.
No, thinner,
a fragility.

Stroking her hair, thick & coarse, gray & red.
Her face dusted with perspiration & the thick gargling
of mucous in her lungs welling out, air drawing in.
Inside her body shutting down her organs parting from their tasks,

"it's not your turn,
there is a lake to walk to, there is water to walk along."

Describing the lake we'd walk to.

So inside herself she has no knowing.

I think of an insect — that fly — trapped inside the stained
globe of *darlingtonia,* its spotted translucency,
light entering from so many angles & none of them true.

For six months she has been up & down &
I have not charted it, not kept track of the progress
& what I saw because I did not want to be
charting her dying.

That sick — I think you will die first.

But I could have an accident.
Your death —
imminent, understood,
so imposing that

as long as I can die first
I can insist on the distance

between your *dying*
& your *death*.

       Easy for me to say

Her eyes were open, she was following me with her sticky eyes.
I asked the nurse to clean them.
I stroked her forehead, played with her hair.
I said to her, "Shirley, I'm playing with your hair."

There is that sweet smell
at your bed that leaves
the imprint of my teeth
in the flesh of my hand.

Afraid my finger

                      would break through her skin.

I had to look. Even from where I stood in the hall outside her door the skin was wrong. Someone said something about *the body*.

Then someone said something about *changing the sheets*.

I stared I could not believe that she could be that dead I could not put that person with the person I knew.

Vulnerable, with no vanity, no Shirley left in her,
utterly other, utterly not here anymore & so she is
invulnerable.

passed
away

Strangeness arranges itself around her. A pair of glasses on the bedside table.

At night you visit, slack-jawed gaunt impaled
on my imagination.

She wouldn't let go until someone said to her *you can*

let go now.

Now I understand *well up*,   how
if I touch it with my mind, my eyes —

Her death as if she owned it.

She *met her death* as if it were a thing outside her coming toward her, arm
extended & she took it, she took the thing inside her self & it was hers. *Became
her*

It wasn't — pretty,   they didn't make her look pretty.
Didn't close her mouth or comb her hair or tuck
the covers up to hide how thin she was. She *was*

                                        put to rest

How strange it is how swiftly she retreats

and this is what happens when I try to say how death is ——
how it settles on the lips, enters the shining mouth.

Letter

How are you? I hate to ask. I got your nails.
The old man at Winks who couldn't find them found them
on a back shelf. He called them *infinitesimal.*
They are for someone I said who mounts endangered
butterflies on velvet-covered coreboard
because he wants something beautiful that won't get away against a backdrop
that will keep him from valuing the whole thing over much.
Then I had another thought. I didn't write it down and I lost it.
That's the way I am now.
What is the social context of cells?

Today it snowed so I read about the bower bird though cause
and effect is mostly tenuous like today and yesterday
but get this, the bower bird picks blue
to make its nest. Blue this, blue that.
The object attends but, really,
weather's what's interesting.
Every time it just sits down to what it is.
When the call came to come in, talk in person
it must have added up. That mock-bronchial cough.
The day's terminal
appointment   shit
I almost envy you almost
knowing where you
locate the infinite.   Sick!
I'm afraid of what you'll miss John.
Of missing you. Today Jeff said of a moment
in a poem I wrote, "I hate those canned moments in second person direct address
when the reader knows it's him who is really being addressed. Romantic!"
Does your life feel different, the way immediately you know

when the tunnel is no longer France, it has become Italy?
That darkness isn't the same and the train rumbles
the tracks with a different racket. What I can't ask you
couldn't tell me. The darkness
is the same. Write soon. Forgive me
when I use you.
Holding his cup of mucous, cells, erratica, pus, what else?
Then something-other's clumsy-handed someone and it spills.

M

Conjunctions

for J. P.

just

after, when respiration had quit —

she stuck   , *thrust*

the vacuum cleaner's hose

head down his throat

                                        to

suck him   out

and he could breathe again it didn't

last   and he exclaimed

        do it again, ohhhhh baby!

while he had air, a joke.   it was a joke.

Drive

It must have seemed to him a sign of his secret
health that he could drive into the city to pick up
his friend who'd flown in to see him off
for what more clearly signifies vitality than a stream
of cars until they become *traffic*, rushing over asphalt
each to its singular destination — interview, date — any event
suggesting a going-on but also a possible
opening-up, life swerving — new job, new love, piling up
unforeseen signs and exits all
with *the rest of my life* in front
that mostly we prefer to call *forever*, as in
"I will love you forever."

So when he pulled up to the *pick up*
passenger zone I was unprepared
for his glow. I expected *terminal*
to have tamped him down, sallowed his skin
but he was so much the same
John I couldn't imagine then how he could get from how he looked to
dead in the time they gave him.

It must have seemed to him I was just along for the ride.
My life was without weight so we could fly
past triple-length trucks in the girdle grip of a viaduct
that spit us out on the high flat tail
of a bus. I couldn't say *slow down* and rise
to reveal my pettiness. The matter was delicate.
Nothing to lose, much, he must have thought
he would show me just how
easy it could be.

Ad Infinitum

My long-term goal is the peaches, he'd said.

August is my long-term goal.

So then I couldn't help myself.

Real Life #11: Hummingbird

Postponement is my opiate but John's the opposite. He coughs and what he spits
into his cup looks like eggwhite between frothy and forms-

a-stiff-peak. *Look at that hummingbird*, he points. Distraction is meant to be

contagious. Already he's apologetic. Embarrassed by what his body does; there is

no bird outside the window.

                                                  There are three cups on the table:

coffee (mine) eggnog (his) And in the other one? He has some names for it —

lung-latté   lung-butter   phlegm-fudge   cream-pus   *Here is your life,*

is the cup half filled? But I don't say it. When the cup's filled he empties it.

After the *he said, I said*, I asked, he hedged.   After he stopped I stopped.
After he paused I asked, he turned.   I asked.   After he died.

John Is in the Next Room

John is in the next room.

The dead man I sit beside who keeps the house up until all hours.

How late is that is a question.

That he is still is to be expected and that he is still
John is a surprise.

At the edge of his lip I see a puddle of saliva tremble
that would fall were he to move. It is too obvious to mention that moving
is beyond him.

And the thing will slip
of its own generative mass with a viscosity that promises it will lengthen
as it falls,

suture a wet lip to a clean shirt.

The glistening extension snaps. But before that my tongue is close
enough to touch it.

John is in the next room.

Inscape

Add
Infinitum.
Ad
Infinitum.
Add in
Finitum:
Infant
Item. Ad in fini
Tum.
To that ad
Blue has a quorum. But green has the meadow.

Echo to Narcissus

Nature drives me crazy, how it repeats.
Yet I love pattern as I love a promise,
to think that what will follow is something
I can know. How ring for ring the oak grows.
And I in felling it repeat the blows. Narcissus,
pattern weds us. And he says "no."

She answers *no.*

Real Life #14: Vagaries

How it began —
Invented in the paroxysms of habit by unmilked women and pale men.
That existence was invented? Who invented a language to make existence felt?
Babbling in so many tongues like toads on a summer pond, deep evening, the sky
going under to the night. And the supper-seeking frogs tonguing the air,
their smoothest resilient lover. Here language began on the tongues of those
seeking sustenance on the fading evening, on the little deaths that were
the answers to the music the evening offered. How invisible he could be.

It went on —
How he could hardly talk to anyone or ask any questions, as if he were waiting
for permission but there wasn't anyone who could give it to him. He suffered
a chronic urgent furtive anxious eagerness to not bother anyone, to cast
    no shadow,
not disturb the air he breathed. And it only made him more conspicuous.
It only gave him an air of perpetual anxiety, as if he stood in the check-out
    line in front
of a long line of shoppers. He was scrambling in his pockets for cash
    and his money
had come up short and he had to put something back. But what?
He scrounged in his pockets and sweated in the heat of his own overabundant
apologies to the shuffling line growing at his back.

How it ended & went on —
He lifted the utensil to his mouth, opening his mouth.
The mouth was open already in anticipation: parted: between
the arm that raised the fork and the mouth that parted an understanding
passed: receiving: this

is the body's function because something's always leaving. Like them
he's in the first person. Constructed of consequence
and as if that's not enough he can see it in the garden, in how the blossom-
burdened floribunda understands extravaganza, post-   *mortem.*

Woman Sitting for a Portrait at a Warehouse Sale

—— Sweeping her broad here, narrow there, feathering her
brow with an astonishment
of charcoal, giving her mouth motive, now
tearing the gloss into likeness and not.
Her face is shut, her lines are slim.
Her lines are scratchy, at drifted angles
like beachtown shanties after the storm's swept in.
What blooms on her chest blooms
also in her hair. That way she echoes red,
that self-containment.

Something inside her has climbed a cliff overlooking,
yes, the ocean. She is what
the water breaks on. Far off,
harbor seals slump on rocks.
They are small and she wants them.
She cannot see their heads without remembering
their secret bodies. She sits for him,
he gives his name to her
imperfect likeness.

Sonnet

The threatened vernal pool fairy shrimp is a ³/₄-inch
translucent crustacean with a one-year life cycle
and a unique survival strategy.

Invisible in vernal pools ——
the fairy shrimp have no secrets.
But if their bodies are —— in water ——
as transparent as desire what
can desire hold?
This close to bodiless —— what they possess
they will not have and what's seen-
through seems only there by her
imagining them. So that later
when his fingers touched her navel ——— *I'll kiss you*
there, only —— is what he said and let his mouth roam
up to where the quartermoon of one breast
quieted him, she could feel how he had practiced
this before with his eyes closed   and alone.

The Mathematics of Fire

The man who bends like a paper clip
to plant a forest of snuffed matches
at his feet can thus do at once

two things. Furthermore,
he can hold four
lit cigarettes in his mouth, then

eight. Puff.
For him to eat them
makes us all look

a little sick. The
length one man will go
to for a quarter is equal

or unequal to the length
of time we can stand
to watch him? Passersby

walk into traffic to get past us,
we absorb them. Knot
in the rope, clot

in the bloodstream. . . . When he draws
a breath I know a man
can make himself so narrow

nothing slips through. The crowd
sucks itself in. He holds the crowd
and it thickens around him. How

many flames can one man consume?
We are his nourishment too.

Feathers

This dog's mouth is eager with feathers.
This dog's mouth is eager with the warm feathers.
I saw the dog haul out
of the weeds the unbitten
bird and started having second thoughts.
There's something in there I want to talk about.
Eager with the feathers
of the just dropped bird,
that dog's mouth inside is empty.
Now I don't want to.
And this dog's
mouth is what I think of
when I think of you when I don't want to.

Early Romance: Japanese Garden *(in the heart of the city)*

We sit on a bench & look at the raked rocks:
The islands of Japan. The improbable waves.

The sculptor muses on his black-billed magpie

I don't know
that I can take
the magpie apart anymore
or speak for you
although I love you well
enough to hear
your argument. I will admit
to a tenderness
I want to resist,

as I want to abstract
the bird, eviscerate it
to its essential   *mag*,   to nothing
less than a talon's grasp.
I would instead place the wing down
there, dispatch the beloved
whole.   I hear myself

I want   I want   I want.   I am
afraid
to sleep with you. For the last years
of my marriage my breathing
disturbed my wife's sleep. Here
is the bird. As apart
as I can make it.

Valediction
for Claudia

And if she can not turn back without turning
To stone, to silence, to say *Dearly*

Departed, I am leaving, turn of the mind, the heart's
Rearrangement

With the past, still it must be hard
To feel that it is not wrong to turn.

Love sipped through the bent straw.
Love set on a shelf where the light

Hits it, unfaltering
Sense that *the little things*

Don't *just add up*.
Or Orpheus

At the tunnel's lip, sliding
Into the brilliant loss

Of uncertainty.
Now seeing is what's new.

The cradle of shared memory
Has cracked. He wants her back;

She has her back
To him. First

To herself
She'll think

What's wrong is newly what I do discard

Fragment's Song

That I might wander into longing,
might witness the fragrant tears, tears of blood, myrrh or miraculous
oils — but this one wept blood.
In the chapel in drifted rows —
and only the icon was looked on
for if we were too, why wouldn't I know it?

That I might wander into longing
what would you spend? remark? — to keep
unfilled? I would not mind the taking measure.
Or leave without recalling why the single white spirea
bent beyond its own doubling by the gray wall
by the rain that filled whatever cavity allowed it in
that night. Nor break by weight of what by some account
is shaken out.

Moon Casings

The full moon is not beautiful
and the headaches when her head
was bent that way
proved matter less stable than we thought.
The full moon that could tell —
could swell with meaning — until the order of words
failed in her.

       There's how it got there —
how it got to gather mass and be intruder
who might occlude cognition. Balance
would fail her. The full moon tells a story,
a chronology of movement
toward the center and out again.
The children — who have no name
for it — draw pictures —

       Moon upon moon — we are drawn
into the dense and glowing center, cast
there at the white shore of cells,
the location of where she is where
there is no backwards and no
future and the nurses were kind
to warn her when it was slivered out
she would hear inside her head the sound of it
assuming the very shape of
things at the edge throw the edge
into dispute and suggest something beyond
the full moon is not beautiful and the rind —

slim moon — the surgeon left
might not possess that critical
mass it needs to rise
again — he says — *leaving
all things aside* —

Map

Everywhere there was a bush and a bird in it.
Things popped out of the grasses
clicking and you knew
you were walking in nature, entering Brush Canyon
exiting Bird so I kept thinking why
should I be the one always asking where it hurts?
Somewhere we paused where
a plank got wedged between trees,
tight so we could sit on it. I touched the wound
— that something viscous
could be pitch at an attitude that hard.
Where Bird Canyon was subsumed by Bear Gulch
the one I was with peeled off to shortcut up some shortcut
so I walked up Downey Gulch through a saw of indolent cows.
I knew them for what they were — red eyes, bulk
and jitteriness —
the way it's always something.
For the first time it was clear to me
that the lines on my map were the draws
and gullies I was lost in
so I couldn't stay lost. That night the sky was nothing
but stars and the crickets made a curtain of sound.
Why can't I remember that? He washed my hair.
I lay on the porch with my neck extended; he rested
my head in his open hand. The sky had rounded
up all its citizens and pressed down.

Historic House, Astoria

I was there for the invention of nostalgia.
It wasn't for everyone and never would be
though the view has changed. Freighters
lining the channel on their way
upriver to the other city, these were the past.
It isn't the room I want but the view from out the window.
The doors and knobs disclose the probable height of the owners and
from their bunks at night sailors could smell the trees
from miles off shore. Back then the future was far away
but when you get there
it's just as big as what you left
though some of the details have been lost.
Someone had to go far into the community,
bringing back breadboards all circa the same
until the house is more as we imagine it than how it was.
It wasn't my old life I wanted but the one that had eluded me.
I examine the roundness of nooks and mantels.
Side-buttoning white shoes.
The trees are small because the weather's hard
though feet in general have grown in length
and spread over
the past 100 years.

Happy

All the years he ate, marrying
flesh to flesh until what should cradle
organs binds them. The body fuses, grows
diffuse and the flesh makes its own
topography indifferent to muscle and bone.
Now when he must be turned she turns him.
Everything gets stacked and there are new creases.
The body makes its own weather, odor.
The way fog settles in.
Until a clumsiness ensues, that movement
should emerge from amplitude.

What space there is between the parts
is half a whisper, a rubbing when he walks, when
he *could* walk. Now anything he wants must
come to him for he can't meet it.
She thinks what she can do for him.
Thinks *think what you like but don't say it*.
Makes the children quiet
down. Makes everything a labor
though for a long time the feet remain
delicate and there is so much softness
it begins to look like happiness.

The Fecundity

Showing nothing of what it hid invited the women to enter.

Part the leaves, tuck through the branches.

Under/inside the weeping beech was a wraith of limbs.

The women saw where it touched the ground it rooted.

Where it touched itself it cleaved.

That it could make an unbroken circle of a single thick branch ——

this was architecture!

One woman uttered grotesque ("Oh, the monstrosity of self-generation!")

The other reveled in the monstrosity ("Oh, the fecundity of grief!")

It turned out the inside

was nothing like the outside &

it turned out that the truth was thrilling & what was thrilling

also was vegetable.

Home

He entered her
took up
residence

some-
what the way
a small animal
lives
& dies &
leaves a cavity
the shape
exactly

The Infinite Imperative

The notion of infinity had its day but you
were beautiful and so far from me that the notion
of notion hardly existed as a place to rest
my head, a singular ledge upon which the flowers might dry
to a more exquisite because more fragile design.

The notion of infinity excites and quiets me
but it is largely the sound of snow stinging the one eye,
blind as it is, scanning the horizon out of habit, that brings me back.
Description doesn't do it for me as you can see.
But here's a rough sketch.   And now I see how the past hangs
upside down in the cage of its muscled feathers
and that the world you would enter is best
seen through a single hole large enough
for a single eye to fill it.

Lament

Where the hole's been cut

small rocks exposed, embedded, suspended as if floating or caught by
    surprise on their way —
where would they be going?

Emma's gone.

And the roots of weeds that had been hidden all this time   ripped and all
    over up and down
the hole's flanks the haphazard scrape-marks
of the shovel.

I want to stand where I can see the hole is overheard and a woman moves
out of the shade into the sunshine.

Emma's gone.

When her father drives the first shovel into the mound of dirt and
    drops his burden
onto the casket
that is the most futile sound.

A body lost at sea is *a subject unattended in the waves.*

Emma is attended

although even her father said, "I don't like the earth much now either."

Home Is a Stone House

Is the gate closed at the bottom
sounded like *Stay close to papa.*
We three who drive out here to hear her talk now
sit and watch her.
The lettuce is unwashed.
Gil left her
and she climbed 3-Fingered Jack,
anchored her bedroll to the flattest spot
and hung that night. Then Broken Top.

In her loss and loneliness she watched
the birds below her.   Raptors.   Odd,

      that god should be placed
above and not just   *elsewhere.*

Successive hills took on a graduation,
not fainter,

quite, but lighter.
The distance calmed her.

Hummock of bivouac contained her body like a sac.
She could lean back into nothing

and still be there.

The rocks are just the way I left them she says
so we look.
Watch her flick the shiny inched-up-to-a-hunch-

back bug out the threshold.
It drop, her pick it up and fling it out into the social
bunchgrass.

The Iowa Poetry Prize and Edwin Ford Piper Poetry Award Winners

1987
Elton Glaser, *Tropical Depressions*
Michael Pettit, *Cardinal Points*

1988
Bill Knott, *Outremer*
Mary Ruefle, *The Adamant*

1989
Conrad Hilberry, *Sorting the Smoke*
Terese Svoboda, *Laughing Africa*

1990
Philip Dacey, *Night Shift at the Crucifix Factory*
Lynda Hull, *Star Ledger*

1991
Greg Pape, *Sunflower Facing the Sun*
Walter Pavlich, *Running near the End of the World*

1992
Lola Haskins, *Hunger*
Katherine Soniat, *A Shared Life*

1993
Tom Andrews, *The Hemophiliac's Motorcycle*
Michael Heffernan, *Love's Answer*
John Wood, *In Primary Light*

1994
James McKean, *Tree of Heaven*
Bin Ramke, *Massacre of the Innocents*
Ed Roberson, *Voices Cast Out to Talk Us In*

1995
Ralph Burns, *Swamp Candles*
Maureen Seaton, *Furious Cooking*

1996
Pamela Alexander, *Inland*
Gary Gildner, *The Bunker in the Parsley Fields*
John Wood, *The Gates of the Elect Kingdom*

1997
Brendan Galvin, *Hotel Malabar*
Leslie Ullman, *Slow Work through Sand*

1998
Kathleen Peirce, *The Oval Hour*
Bin Ramke, *Wake*
Cole Swensen, *Try*

1999
Larissa Szporluk, *Isolato*
Liz Waldner, *A Point Is That Which Has No Part*

2000
Mary Leader, *The Penultimate Suitor*

2001
Joanna Goodman, *Trace of One*
Karen Volkman, *Spar*

2002
Lesle Lewis, *Small Boat*
Peter Jay Shippy, *Thieves' Latin*

2003
Michele Glazer, *Aggregate of Disturbances*
Dainis Hazners, *(some of) The Adventures of Carlyle, My Imaginary Friend*